i had a
brother
once

i had a brother once

a poem, a memoir

adam mansbach

one world
new york

Copyright © 2021 by Giants of Science, Inc.

Published in the United States by One World, an imprint of Random House, a division of Penguin Random House LLC, New York.

ONE WORLD and colophon are registered trademarks of Penguin Random House LLC.

LIBRARY OF CONGRESS CATALOGING-IN-PUBLICATION DATA
Names: Mansbach, Adam, author.
Title: I had a brother once : a poem, a memoir / Adam Mansbach.
Description: New York : One World, [2021]
Identifiers: LCCN 2020031115 (print) | LCCN 2020031116 (ebook) | ISBN 9780593134795 (hardcover ; acid-free paper) | ISBN 9780593134801 (ebook)
Subjects: LCSH: Grief—Poetry. | LCGFT: Poetry.
Classification: LCC PS3613.A57 I3 2021 (print) | LCC PS3613.A57 (ebook) | DDC 811/.6—dc23
LC record available at https://lccn.loc.gov/2020031115
LC ebook record available at https://lccn.loc.gov/2020031116

Printed in the United States of America on acid-free paper

oneworldlit.com

9 8 7 6 5 4 3 2 1

First Edition

Book design by Caroline Cunningham

Title page and interlude image: iStock/traffic_analyzer

i had a
brother
once

first of all i never

usually stayed out past

midnight or even ten,

but i was feeling

myself that night.

something was ending

& it was time to celebrate.

my friend emery had

reserved the back room

of a center city lounge

so we could spin some

records for the first &

final time before i

packed up the rented

carriage house &

u-hauled out of town.

one year in philly had

sprawled into two &

i'd been digging weekly

that whole time

at this spot called beautiful

world & another called

milkcrate, plus mark's

spot, which didn't have

a name, & then there was

another out past bryn mawr

that i found by accident,

a place the local deejays

had long written off

as trash, except i happened

to fall through just as

a new collection came up

from the basement, had not

even been filed yet, all

holy grail joints—the del

jones record, a mint

original headless heroes

of the apocalypse lp,

the bo diddley with the

break, the rhetta hughes,

the johnny houston, some

forty pieces & nothing

stickered past eight bucks.

it's bound to happen if

you dig long & doggedly

enough, but only about

once per decade. my last two

had been waterville maine

in ninety-six & the jamaican

lady i met outside academy

records in manhattan double

parked on twelfth street,

truck sagging with roots

reggae. there were two guys

working that day, a bald

headed whiteboy & a dread,

& the wrong one jogged out.

he took a quick flip through

& passed. i slid up & i asked

if i could look, ended up

jumping in the shotgun seat

& driving back up to the bronx

to see what she had left at home.

that was two thousand two

or possibly oh-three

& now it was may twenty-eight

two thousand eleven. i'd

amassed two crates, one for

each year of my expiring

university appointment, &

barely listened to a lot of it

myself; all i had at the house

was a portable turntable emery

had let me hold, & all my

three year old wanted to hear

was the dixie cups crooning

about their trip to the chapel

of love, maybe because her

mother & i were not

married ourselves.

i had not spun out

since leaving california, &

music always sounds different

when you are rocking for

a room, studying the way

each song hits. deejaying

is the art of making people

hear what you do. each

record transforms the crowd

& each crowd the record.

i invited my grad students

& most of them came. it

was a small mfa program,

tightknit, with little of the

pettiness or gamesmanship

i recalled from my own.

after workshop we often

went for drinks, a motorcade

of hatchbacks & tin cans

cruising four blocks to the

tavern near campus because

walking even that far was

considered foolhardy in

camden at night. one bar

for an entire university was

one too few, meant i risked

seeing my undergrads

drunk, but it was no worse

than running into them while

i was lifting weights at the

school gym, & for the most

part we were all adept at

not getting in each other's

way, like housemates sharing

a kitchen.

somebody took a flick

of me behind the wheels

that night, probably leslie.

my left hand is pressed

to the wax, fingertips

backcuing the funky

little drumfill at the top

of hit or miss, right hand

a jutting peace sign,

elbow cocked, arms tan,

emery grinning beside me.

that was one of the last

records i played, which

means it was about twelve

thirty & might even be after

the first call from my father,

the one i ignored, straight

cognitive dissonance, there

was no earthly reason

he would call that late &

i was in the middle of

my set, no one was sick

or frail, my last living

grandparent was already

dead. i told myself

he must have dialed by

mistake in his car, home

bound from the newspaper

after writing the first headline

the greater boston area would

see tomorrow when they freed

the globe from its plastic

sheath, tipped their coffee

mugs mouthward, destroyed

the symmetry of their donuts.

but five minutes later

he called again & this time i

picked up, cupping a palm

over my open ear to blunt

the funk booming behind.

i still didn't think anything

was wrong. in fact, i remember

or think i remember being

slightly annoyed, in the belief

that this call was a frivolous

intrusion, which makes

so little sense that perhaps

i knew better & was frightened

enough to erect this cardboard

buttress.

my father said

i've put this off as

long as possible

that's not what he said.

i mean me. i would live

here in this preamble

forever. rework it. fold in

new ingredients. knead it

till the gluten breaks. yammer

on about records. tell some

jokes. have i mentioned

that on this night & for

the six weeks beforehand

a book i had written that

did not yet technically exist,

could not be held in hands till

june, was somehow outselling

every other book in the world?

there was almost certainly

a split second when i

convinced myself my father

was calling about that,

jubilant with some new

tidbit that had dropped into his

newsroom off the a.p.

wire, additional victims

claimed by this viral sensation

of mine. we could talk about

the book. i could tell you

a few stories about stories,

flip a little wordplay, we could

warm up with some improv

games. it has been eight

fucking years & i have written

everything but this.

my father said
david has taken his own life

& i answered as if i didn't

understand or hadn't heard.

my reply was *what?* & he

repeated it. there is plenty

to regret & perhaps this

is insignificant but i wish

i had not made him

say it to me twice.

the second time i was in

motion, walking through the

back room, the front room,

out into the heatwave night.

i wasn't crying yet but i also

couldn't speak or think.

my father's sentence was

unrecognizable, a cluster of

words spinning in a void.

the notion that it was all

a mistake flashed through me

& fell instantly to ash.

no parent would say such

a thing about his child

to his child if there was any

hope. & here begins a different

kind of struggle, on this

page, akin to keeping the

steering wheel perfectly

straight, a struggle not

to crane out of this shot, not

to add voiceover, not

to do the one thing i am

trained to, which is make

things legible, impose

structure & plot, motivation,

a frame, a double helix of

narrative to snake through

the spine, to be the spine.

here i am, here we are,

not fifty feet from the news

of my brother's suicide &

already i can feel a tug at

the reins. i don't know if

naming these things can

sap their power or if it

constitutes a sacrifice

at their altar, an invitation

to the impulse i am trying

to disperse. what are

the rules of this endeavor,

am i supposed to unfold

the moments of this night

like an origami crane,

crease by crease, is that

the penance or the healing,

the ritual, a march toward

or away from what? penance

for what? if you are making

up the ritual as you go,

is it a ritual? if the loss is

a hole that cannot be filled,

is the remainder of your

life the ritual? are rituals

supposed to fill the hole or

deepen it until you can

crawl out the other side,

& who am i that i have

to ask? my mother's mother's

father's parents were the

children of famed rabbis,

they came here & founded

a jewish community

in burlington vermont by

paying other jews to keep

the sabbath, making them whole

& a minyan by handing out

the wages they would have

lost in observing the holy day,

& here i am not even a hundred

& fifty years later, acting as if

the books my people carried

& died for are unknown to me.

here i am freighted by nothing,

reinventing the wheel, reinventing

the rack. daring to believe

that perhaps you only realize

a ritual was one after

you complete it, inscribe the

final character. a tear falls

on the page, becomes

the final period or some

stupid maudlin shit like that.

i don't know what more

my father said right then. i

hung up, walked back inside

somehow, told emery i had

to go, told him my brother

was dead, felt something

of the horror come into focus

when i read it on his face.

he asked me what i needed,

offered to drive me home, but

i said no, just, i don't know,

take my shit when you leave,

& i walked out through the

front door again & called

my father back, but not right

away, i think. first i stood

talking to my brother.

david, what did you do?
david, what have you done?

i haven't gotten past that, have

received no answer, have not

felt him lingering, not even

then, not like when my grandfather

died & the thunderstorm came or

my grandmother died &

a month of nightmares

about her staggering vacant

& drooling through the halls of

her summer house followed.

no, my brother had chosen

to go & was gone, utterly

gone, was not nearby, was not

available in any way i could discern,

& i was crying too hard to see now,

walking through badly blurred

streets toward my car. i called

my father back. he was with

my mother, of course, they

were at david's apartment

with his wife. widow.

david had been missing

all day & they had feared that

he would not come back,

but only just now had his body

been discovered, in his car,

he was a scientist, had done it

by mixing two chemicals

into a gas that killed him

painlessly, with a single

breath. he'd left a note

on his windshield warning

of the toxic fumes inside so

no one else would die, but

i did not learn that until later.

what i learned then was that

there was, had been, a secret

& that secret was death, the

want of death. his wife had

kept it for him, fasted, prayed,

she was catholic, from a catholic

country, she placed her faith

in self-denial & fervent whispered

words, believed they held

the power to restore him

to himself, or maybe she just

didn't know what else to do.

david forbade her to tell

anyone that he cried in dark rooms,

held his head between his hands,

his hands between his knees,

did not want children, refused

to put another person through

that, that being childhood,

that being life. i could not

even conceive of a word like

forbade describing david.

he was too gentle, his hands

were large & powerful but

looked most natural holding

puny things, gripping a carrot
& a peeler or splaying an
eyelid & squeezing a dropper
from above. but no one is
gentle with the things they
fear or the people who
discover them unmade.
she kept his secrets until
she could not, then told
my parents, who did not
tell me. we are a family
conditioned to believe
depression is something
you live with, as ben did,
as philip did, as marion did,
as j & i & a do, &
not something that kills you,
but we were wrong. the
not telling me is gnarled,

leaves me both furious

& grateful, & ashamed

to be either. it closes one

set of parentheses & opens

another, tenders me an alibi

& lets a myth of thwarted

salvation take furtive root.

by now my father was telling

me that i should not be driving

in this condition & i was

promising not to as i merged

onto the highway, on my way

home, where i knew i would

have to wake up v & break

the news, the world.

that final moment is what i

dwell on most. he is sitting

in his subaru, overlooking

nothing, the ass end of

a parking lot, those fucking

chemicals lying in his lap,

knowing he is one breath

away, that he could end it

all right now, though any

of us could, really, it is

always right now, there are

always heights & cars, things

to fling yourself off or in

front of, there is always

a drawer full of knives.

i imagine he is crying, but

that is only because i would be.

perhaps he is laughing, or

luxuriating in the sudden

vivid crispness of the world,

the miraculous dispersal of

cumulonimbus formations

in a southwesterly wind, &

feeling free at last, or

just as likely he is stone

faced with determination, so

close, just one final push.

perhaps the act was a ritual,

a series of gestures rehearsed

& enacted with faithful,

reverent precision, the

implements delicate in his

large hands like eyedroppers,

carrot peelers. it is all

unfathomable. i cannot

place myself in him. i'm

throwing clichés at the wall.

they say a velvet calm descends

when people have decided,

gathered their supplies, chosen

a place, an hour. their moods

lighten & their loved ones think

they've turned a corner, which

they have. a different corner.

but in my head that's where

he always is, sitting in his car

with me screaming *don't do it*

from the back seat like some

spirit cursed to be unheard.

& my mother's mother's

father's parents, the famous

rabbis' kids, the minyan-makers

of burlington vermont, they

squat atop the glass floor

of the distant beyond, shaking

their great woolly heads &

asking why of all things

did it have to be gas.

the last face i made

a mirror of that night

was just a glimpse,

a woman in her stoplit car

as i jaywalked my own

busy street, heedless of

traffic. i knifed past &

she gave me the look you

give the deranged, the

drugged husks, when they

lope too close, an involuntary

response to a musk of misery

so abject & raw that it screams

danger, anything could happen.

i fumbled open the front

door of the crumbling

carriage house & began

climbing the stairs to the

second floor. i have no idea

what banshee sounds i was

making as i walked but

the noise was deliberate. i

dreaded waking v, dreaded

saying the words, & this

would at least serve as

a kind of warning, would

flush her from the bedroom

we shared with our daughter.

she woke & flew out onto

the landing in a panic, *what,*

what's wrong, & i said it,

my brother killed himself,

& it became somehow

even more true.

we collapsed together

on a rug, first wailing &

then crying in many different

ways, i don't know the names

for all of them or if they all

have names. in between,

we flailed at comprehension,

probed weakly at how

everything was different now.

at some point soon before

my body shut down & i slept,

a thought came that felt true,

or maybe it seemed precious

for being the only thought left,

a single green shoot growing

in a razed & barren field,

so i said it: *we have to have*

another baby. if anything

could save my parents, it

would be that. it turned out
to be sort of true, as true as
something like that can be,
but not for years & not with
her & not at all.

emery drove me to the airport
in the morning. v did not come
to boston, did not want little
vivien to see everyone she loved
hysterical with grief, did not
believe you should lean on
your children in that way,
told me it was not a three
year old's job to comfort
anyone, or everyone. i
did not agree, did not think
i could get through this
without her, my daughter

i mean, but i had to go,

i had to go right now.

on the curb, emery asked

if he could pray for me &

i said yes & meant it. he

grabbed both my shoulders,

bowed his head. it began

heavenly father. i'd never heard

anyone make up a prayer

before; in judaism that is called

forgetting the words. the way

he asked the lord to give me

strength was so earnest &

so fierce, so pure, it felt like

the opposite of everything

i'd ever known, his faith

a suit cut from a single bolt

of sheer white linen &

my outfit a ragpicker's

patchwork sewn by

cantankerous & ancient

men. laz picked me up

on the other side & i

rolled down the window

& keened into the highway

wind, maybe hoping to empty

myself & greet my parents

before filling up again.

laz & i met when we were

vivien's age, a pair of toddlers

named adam with baby brothers

named david, & from nursery

school through twelfth grade

we were adam l & adam m,

david l & david m. his family

kept the sabbath & turned

off the ringer at eight thirty

every night & said i love you

to each other all the fucking

time, & in these ways they were

not just our döppelgangers

but our superiors. laz had been

at my grandfather's funeral nine

months earlier, had watched

beside me as the simple pine

box with the star of david

singed into the sides descended

by degrees into a dark pit

fresh cut from the loam &

the entire purpose of this

oldest & most universal

ritual revealed its purpose,

which was not providing

succor through the return

of the beloved to the earth

from whence, but jolting any

fool lingering outside the basest

& most desperate grief back

to his senses, exploding

the benedictions, setting

the eulogies aflame, burning

off the contemplation of

the ineffable by showing him,

showing me, that this was it,

this was death, the box

with the corpse inside

disappears & the ground

closes above it, &

no matter how long you

stand there nothing else is

going to happen. laz &

my brother & i tore off

our suits right afterward,

put on our other suits &

went bodysurfing as the storm

swept in, the rain dartlike &

the waves gray & wind-slanted,

disordered, crashing over

our heads & sweeping our

legs out from beneath us

with relentless truculence,

the way they had when we

were kids & a current of

real danger underlay each

mission into the shallows,

each of us trying to be the last

to walk out of the water &

david, as always, with the most

stamina, the warmest blood.

i had spoken at the service

& david had listened. i had

assumed i spoke for him, that

it was my role to write & speak

on behalf of our generation

when the aged died, but now

it was impossible to know

what he'd been thinking.
had he waited for ben to go,
the way michael waits until
after their mother's funeral
to kill fredo? it seemed to
make sense, felt obscurely
impossible that david could
die while ben still lived,
but then so was all of this.
surely i was not caterwauling
in the shotgun seat of my
oldest friend's dad's car
while my broad-shouldered
younger brother, who'd
scored a perfect sixteen
hundred on his s.a.t. &
graduated his ph.d.
program with honors, who
had a wife & a new job &

could stand indefinitely on

his hands & wore shorts to

all but the most somber

occasions & spent high

school listening to his

weather radio, stormchasing

nor'easters up & down

the coast of new england,

paddling out to meet the curl

in a piss-warmed wetsuit,

shoveling down rice & beans

in his car after with the radiator

blasting & any intrepid fellow

traveler he might have convinced

to join him half-dead of muscle

fatigue & hypothermia, lay

waiting to be identified, eyes

passed over his body one

last time, a task that would

fall to our father, who reported

afterward, in a voice soft &

without bass, only that

he looked like dave.

my brother would have

turned forty tomorrow.

i think about his kids

sometimes, who they

would have been, whether

having them might have

kept him alive. i think

about ayahuasca, the miracle

entheogenic brain rewiring

depression cure the shamans mix

& serve, how instead

of flying to peru to try it

he did nothing of the sort,

just kept on working, sat

at his desk the day before

he sat in that parking lot,

made no changes, marched

straight toward the camp when

about-facing or stopping cold

or jagging left would have cost

my brother what? nothing costs

anything if you don't intend

to live long enough to pay

your debts. why not go back

to guatemala & surf? but

this is not how a depressed

person thinks. i am imposing

dei ex machina, dumping

out my sack of narrative on

the floor, examining this from

the perspective of someone

who wants to be alive.

imagine a house full of people

& nobody leaves. for days,

at any given time at least

half are in hysterics &

sometimes all of them at

once. the sobs & wails

& nose blowings are

interspersed with wan

or ravenous grazing

of the table covered

in food, whatever has

been brought or sent for,

& conversations that all circle

the drain. my mother slept

on the couch in the den

& when she bedded down

the mourners left. she asked

me if i was depressed, had

ever been depressed.

i said no & she burst into

fresh tears, asked *but*

what if you're lying? &

why not? what if everyone

is harboring a secret wish

to die? who will betray us

next? it was like the way i

could not look up at new

york city skyscrapers after

the attacks without expecting

to see planes fly into them.

we were sitting shiva but

did not know how. instead

of covering the mirrors we

became them.

.

the only time no one cried

was at the funeral, we set up

chairs in the living room

& david's wife's priest spoke.

no one else. that fucking

weirdo was no emery.

at a time when every artifact

& sentence was drenched

with meaning, when everything

& everyone seemed like

a secret & the effort of

parsing it all made my eyes

burn with fatigue, his words

alone meant nothing, fell

from his mouth like brittle

leaves, & turned to powder

when they hit the floor.

i wore a suit & no shoes,

& wondered if my brother's

wife, widow, believed he was

in hell, where her church holds

that the soul spends eternity if

you rob god of his right to

kill you. the rest of us

sat there hoping this was

doing her some good, waiting

for it to end, my father so

scornful of religion he can

hardly bear to enter his own

people's house of worship

for a wedding or bar mitzvah,

& somehow a catholic

priest is telling him about

his son in his own living

room. but he was docile.

what was this to object to?

i slept in the basement

that night, tried to force

myself to watch a movie,

turned on a lighthearted

time travel comedy that

just so happens to open

with a wacky suicide.

my cousin matthew & i

drove to david's apartment

the next morning to retrieve &

dispose of things. we wandered

the rooms, read refrigerator

notes, stared at the wedding

photos on the mantel, the

vacation snapshots in their

glass & wooden boxes

by the bed until david's

expression curdled right

in front of us, his eyes

no longer looking at the

camera but some point

beyond, the passage

of time visible in the

deepening hollows of

his cheeks. everything

we'd missed was right

in front of us. david was

thinking about dying inside

every frame, & his wife's

assiduous documentation

of their history was a plea,

a reminder, an attempt to

make the life they lived

together real. get him to

see it. we logged on to

his computer, found the email

receipt for the chemicals.

he had bought them only

two weeks earlier. perhaps

that was the event horizon, or

perhaps it was neither event

nor horizon. these clues that

were not clues were everywhere,

waterlogging everything, as if

the wave he'd spent his life

surfing had finally broken.

among the items my brother

had purchased after the means

of killing himself was an

expensive skateboard that

had not yet arrived, was still

en route. printed out on his

desk, time stamped a few

days earlier, were directions

to a memorial service for our

grandfather that was not until

july. this set of data staggered

me: the bifurcation of david's

intentions, part of him planning

to live & mourn & skateboard,

the rest of him planning to die.

it was not a toggle switch, they

tell me, not an either/or but a

both at once. no more a paradox

than a train station with two

sets of tracks running in

opposite directions.

the note on his windshield

was not the note. the real note

came to us later, in a hazmat

envelope. i only read it once,

transcribed into an email

by my father. it began

As far back as I can remember, I

have always thought I should be dead.

•

who am i to line break

that sentence, chop it

where i feel the rhythm

lies? i'm sorry for that,

david. but also i am furious.

i don't believe you. i

remember your childhood

too, your sun-warmed

body draped across mine

on the beach where we

returned each summer,

bigger & stronger, where

we bored careful holes in

flat wedges of sand with

our thumbs & first fingers

& named them clantobars,

played running bases & rolled

giggling down the sloping

dune into the ocean to

spring up & battle waves.

i remember you with dandelions

behind your ears in grandma's

garden & another poking from

the waistband of your shorts,

before your round belly

knotted into muscle. your

body was the closest mystery,

so like my own that i

cartographed all our differences,

your nose a mansbach &

mine a kaplan, your back

broader & chest hairier,

your strength deeper set

than mine, honed fighting

water instead of iron.

i remember holding your head

still for the clippers, trying to

clean up the haircut you'd

inflicted on yourself, a prelude

to the night a few years later

when, left alone in the house,

you removed the braces from

your teeth & videotaped

the procedure. mom & dad

had made you get them,

did not take seriously your

objection that it was

forced cosmetic surgery.

they believed you'd thank

them later, but you reclaimed

sovereignty over your body,

for the first but not the final

time. even the orthodontist

had to admit you did a superb

job. you walked dogs to pay

back what they had spent &

your teeth stayed fucked up

for the rest of your life, like

our father's. except now, at

seventy-five, he sports invisaligns,

is making what has long been

crooked straight; time passed

& he changed his mind, as

you cannot. there was glee

in your eyes that evening,

do not tell me otherwise,

you bobbed atop your mischief,

grinning with those wires

extruding wildly from your face

like broken walrus whiskers

& the sterilized nail clippers

waving in your hand. &

what about the year you

swallowed daily capsules of

resveratrol, the magic

grape skin compound you

said increased longevity in

rats? i don't believe you,

your last words are lies,

i hereby accuse you, too,

of laying a false frame over

your life, putting braces on it.

but i don't know for sure, i can

prove nothing, am testifying

only to my own blindness,

or your skill at hiding behind

a mask.

the note was short, very

short & very polite. it

seemed almost to elide

the point. there is that first

sentence, & then a part i don't

remember, & then it ends

I would have succumbed to your love

and would be here still.

i suspect i cannot quote the

fragment that lies between

because it is so vague. it

does not name the thing

that is killing him. my father

the editor, the headline writer,

the master artisan of words,

pointed this out. the phrasing

suggests no awareness of how

this murder will affect those
left behind. this too is said
to be typical. those who take
themselves away are sure
that we will all be better off
without them. they cannot
see past their own mirrors,
have lost the ability to
imagine a world in flux,
capable of becoming any
worse than it already is,
or any better.

how do you mourn someone
who claims he never wanted
life? how can you memorialize
a person who chose oblivion?
such a death has nothing in

common with any other.

it is unnatural, may in fact

be the only thing in the world

that is truly & completely so.

the life force is meant to be

locked in combat with the

death force. we evolved to

survive, we fight for our

lives. my brother switched

sides, turned his back on

all of history. david fought

to die.

& meanwhile, as the house

bulged inchoate with grief &

vinnie packed the contents

of my philly crib & trucked

them up to boston, & v &

vivien went to wait at the

cottage on martha's vineyard

that felicia & ben had passed

down to their four grandsons,

meanwhile the book was

hurtling toward existence.

in two more weeks it would

debut atop the list, this

fourteen stanza fake kids'

story with cusswords on

every page that all the giant

publishers had tried & failed

to buy out from beneath

the tiny one. there was a good

chance it would fizzle before

the summer ended & also a

possibility it would achieve

escape velocity & orbit the

planet in perpetuity. my family

was adamant that the best thing
i could do was everything
anybody asked me to, all the
press & all the travel, starting
with a today show interview
locked in for june fourteen,
pub day. better to occupy
yourself, they said, & didn't
need to add that if i stayed
wallowed in the basement
we all lost again. besides
which, their advice was
always the same: work.
work no matter what
& above all. a boston jew
is nothing without his
puritan work ethic. but
i didn't need convincing.
i was desperate to get

out of there & desperately
ambitious, as i had always
been. i wanted to succeed,
wanted to breathe life into
a mythic version of myself
i had sketched out down
there in that wood-paneled
subterranean room where i'd
once gone to play my music
loud. i wanted to be able
to say *the year my brother*
killed himself, i made
a million dollars. it sounded
like a jay-z lyric in my head:
when tragedy hits we hustle
harder, ball out for the dead
& gone, put down our heads
& earn. we smoke these
cigars not for ourselves

now but for them, our

joy forever tempered but

regardless we must glow,

are duty bound to shine

no matter what it takes.

later in the summer i did

say it, to my friend josh,

both of us floating some

hundred yards off the shore

of a flat ocean, & it sounded

so meaningless i never

uttered it again.

david's mask had rendered

his suffering invisible & now

i needed one of my own.

i kept worrying that some

interviewer would learn about

my brother & ambush me,

which was ridiculous. making

the luckiest asshole in the world

break down on camera is not

in anybody's interest, but

being forced to account for

all the parts of myself at once

terrified me nonetheless.

perhaps i also had some notion,

a superstition almost, that

if tragedy was ever allowed

to step into the winner's circle

triumph would be incinerated.

but the realer fear, the one that

stared back from the mirror

lens of every television camera,

was how i would look to

those who knew, which was

all my people by now.

i had asked sarah & daniel

& torrance to make calls,

to spread the word so that

i would never again be

forced to say it myself.

what would my friends think,

i wondered, watching me

grin & quip with kathie lee

gifford like some sociopath?

what would i think of myself

if the mask did not at least slip?

i watch those interviews now &

try to catch something, see

beneath it. i cannot. you'd

never know that anything

was wrong, & perhaps for

those few minutes nothing

was. i too became a train

station.

.

for the next year, i was always

on the road or on the phone,

or lying on my couch awash

in television, gathering

the strength to leave again.

i answered every question

like no one had ever asked

before. we do not turn into

what we pretend to be, but

what we pretend can still

unmake us. worship the false

idol & tell yourself you are

only playing the game

of survival: how long before

that graven image comes to

mean something, or everything?

how long before we confuse

happiness with distance from
disaster, closure with being
unable to remember?

i do remember a gig in dc
that fall. a public relations
firm brought me out for
a happy hour at a georgetown
restaurant, with passed hors
d'oeuvres & cocktails named
after the book. the company
was owned by a woman who
had gone to my high school.
her name was not familiar,
but she knew me & knew
my brother, was between
my age & his; this connection
had been a part of her pitch.

she was going to ask after

david at some point &

the whole night, as i

told funny stories &

signed books & posed

for photos with my arms

around the bare shoulders

of strangers, i could think

of nothing else. this was

one of the scenarios that

haunted me: blindsiding

someone who was only

making polite conversation,

having to watch eyes

register the news again.

they seated us together

at dinner, & i tried to

steer her away from

the only game we had

to play, the game of who

is where & doing what,

do you remember tasha,

her older brother was

your year, didn't you

date my friend susie

for a minute, do you

still keep in touch with

bujalski, gessen, cho.

i took a stab at falling

into a long, absorbing

discussion with the woman

on my other side, but

i could feel it coming, the

heat prickling my skin,

a churning at the bottom

of the gut, & sure enough,

as the servers cleared away

the remains of a meal i

had not even noticed

eating, my hostess fisted

her hand beneath her chin

& asked *so how is dave,*

i haven't seen him in

forever. & i said *yeah,*

he's doing great, he lives

in brookline with his wife.

a century ago, being born

with bilateral clubfoot meant

you would never walk.

now ten seconds of surgery

can fix it. the achilles tendons

are severed & regrown,

the tiny soft young bones

retrained over the course

of months & then reminded

every night for years.

you learn that your child

has this genetic defect when

a sudden silence fills

the ultrasound room.

the technician stops chit

chatting, adjusts her glasses,

rolls her chair across the

tile, darts out the door. you

sense that certain protocols

are being put into effect &

it cannot be good. the goo

stiffens across the taut

exposed belly of your partner

& you lean forward awkwardly

so that your hands can clasp,

& then a doctor you have

never seen before appears.

later a genetic counselor

ushers you into an office

off the main hallway &

says there is a six percent

chance more is wrong.

the number is icy steep,

no matter that a six percent

likelihood of rain would not

make you reconsider your

picnic. & then there are

decisions to make, fraught

& immediate. do you chance

finding out more, when more

might only confuse you, reveal

snarls in the dna that no one

can explain, that science

has yet to map, that might

mean nothing, or everything?

do you risk peace of mind

via the needle, leech a draw

of amniotic broth when there is

a point-five percent possibility

that the thin metal, entering

the body, kills? no one

cancels a picnic over

half a percent, but this is not

a picnic. & for that matter,

how well do you know

this person, with whom you

are having a baby but have

never before been truly

scared? what could you

forgive, if one of you insisted

on a course of action &

was wrong? if there is

more bad news, what then?

we agreed to err on the side

of knowing too much & were

rewarded, though rewarded is

the wrong word, we did not

earn a goddamn thing & it

would have turned out

the same had we done nothing.

we were lucky, that is all.

the clubfoot was just clubfoot.

the needle did not stab the fetus.

the only true fear i had left

remained inside its dungeon,

shackled to its post. all of this

happened much later. the baby

in question is my second child,

almost nine years younger

than my first. what i am

trying to get at is the way

we emerged from this brief

crucible & quickly realized

how unstrange it was,

that it fazed neither

family nor friends, that

everyone we knew knew

someone who'd had progressive

casting, worn the funny little

boots with the bar, that it

could be discussed beneath

blue skies & would not stain

rooms purple, & all this,

everything about this, is

the opposite of suicide.

no one knows anyone who

killed themselves, or if

they do they are not telling

me. this statistic is no more

plausible than six overpowering

ninety-four, i know, but

there are things we cannot

risk draping with language,

things we silo inside ourselves

or attempt to graft onto other

conversations only to learn

that they won't take. nothing

reminds you of this story,

except as black reminds you

of white, or health of sickness.

even discussions of death,

of depression, provide not

a method of ingress but

a reminder that there are

no bridges to this island.

you must swim. the few

times i have done so

i have been a little

drunk & hours into a first

talk with someone i know

i want to keep. a sense

that i am being dishonest,

that everything is false

until i bare this wound,

takes hold of me. i grow

impatient to find a way,

bore open a point of entry,

my heart throwing off sparks

as if i were working up the

courage to declare

my love. once it is said,

i surprise myself no further.

the narrative slithers toward

me, tongue dancing, tasting

the boozy air as it makes

a caduceus of the barstool leg. the

embers go gray inside me

as i tell the story, deepening

the grooves of the track &

keeping my head down to

avoid seeing the vicious

unexplored terrain scream

past the windows. what

was meant to be a laying

down of armaments,

a call to intimacy, seems

like the opposite now,

calculated, mannered,

weaponized, as if the only

point had been to illustrate

that i, or i too, or i like you,

am seasoned by tragedy,

my flavor made complex.

or maybe it is that i can

feel the tremor of hooves,

see another horde of questions

cresting the hilltop, & i hate

all my answers.

i did know one person: mark,

who owned the nameless

philly record spot, a fourth

floor room in an unheated

steel building, more storage

space than store. he was

open on sundays & by

appointment, & his brother

had killed himself. i was
back in town to give a
talk at my old school, a few
months after david died.
douglas had tipped me off
& so i sought mark out.
my parents had attended
a meeting of suicide
survivors, that is the
tortured, oxymoronic
nomenclature for the
people left behind,
but only once. i had not
even considered it, could
not see any point, knew
or imagined i knew exactly
what it would be like,
everybody sitting in a
circle telling each other

it wasn't their fault &
admitting that they were
angry, or weren't angry
anymore. but mark was
weird & wise, smelled like
loose tobacco & the must
of ages, bought & sold rare
books, & when i had once
asked him what he liked
to read he said memoirs by
pre-twentieth-century
schizophrenics, written
before the existence
of the word, the diagnosis,
any understanding of the
affliction. books by people
who had no idea what
the fuck was happening
to them, whose terrors had

no names or the wrong

names, were blamed on demons

& treated with bloodletting,

who wrote out of desperation,

hoping it might save their lives.

so i told mark & he told me.

it turned out to be not one but

both his brothers. maybe

a parent too, i am ashamed

to say i can't remember.

mark said he understood it,

that his brothers' decisions held

no mystery for him. suicide,

to his way of thinking, seemed

almost an inevitability,

something you got around to

sooner or later, when you had

no fight left in you & the time

was right. i bought some

reggae forty-fives & left

thinking my god, the only thing

worse than not understanding

would be to understand,

to know it like the night

knows darkness.

i came to think of my grief as

bottomless, because nothing

i threw down it made a sound.

it could not be filled so instead

i found some plywood &

walled it off the way one might

a treacherous system of caverns,

scrawled a warning sign & nailed

that up as well. some days i pulled

everything down & peered

over the edge just long enough

to feel the fear of falling that is

really a fear of jumping, &

others i walked by without

a wayward glance. i knew

better than to call this healing,

or disparage it as anything

short of tremendous progress.

the decision to look or

not look, feel or not feel,

took its place among

the rituals of my day,

the espresso & the gym, the

desk & chair, the escalating

fights & bitterness, the plotting

of escape routes, putting

the toddler down for her nap,

not calling my parents.

time is longer than rope but

both can strangle you or

knot themselves beneath

your feet & implore you

to climb.

.

when one puts on a mask,
as david did, as i did, one
does not become another.
one becomes two. the inner
peers through the outer.
the outer feels the blood
pulse from behind. the
dreidel game we play at
hanukkah is a gambling
game & also a lie, invented
at a time, one of many,
when we were forbidden
from study, from prayer,
the two have always been
synonymous to us, & so
we pretended to wager on
the spinning top made
out of clay & became two.
there is a joke about a jew

who buys the house next

door to rockefeller, drives

the same cadillac, hires

the same gardener to edge

the shrubbery, clearly this

jew has spun the dreidel well.

one morning rockefeller

glances across the hedgerow

as the two of them step into

their identical conveyances

& in disgust says *you think*

you're as good as me, don't

you? the jew says *certainly not,*

i think i'm better. rockefeller

demands to know why.

for one thing, the jew explains,

i don't live next door to a jew.

we survive by learning how

the goyim see themselves

& us. this becomes as reflex,

breath, the head jerking toward

the twig snap. what comes less

easily is remembering how

to see ourselves, see as

ourselves, feel the blood pulse

from behind the mask as

we bear witness to that which

seeks to confound eyesight,

scrub itself right out of history,

that which cannot be judged,

not by the likes of us, mere

flies on walls, liminal beings,

necessary evils, middlemen,

landless, unrooted, circum-

scribed, scapegoated

but enough. these masks of ours

are not the heroic disguises

the ancestors wore. ours

do not double consciousness,

ours cut everything in half.

a mask you wear to bed

is no tool of survival,

no matter what task you must

perform when you wake up.

david died in his mask &

perhaps because of it. silence

did him in, & this in its

own way is just as hideously

ironic as the gas. he feared

being known more than he

feared death, refused to do

the thing that makes us human,

which is telling our stories,

claiming & declaiming them,

& so all i can do to grapple

my way back is write his, or

maybe i mean mine, make

ritual of being known as he
would not, build a bridge
to that island or become
one. but what a forced
& tidy resolution this
appears in certain light,
both true & false, profound
& glib, to speak of memory
as life & forgetting as death,
or death as forgetting, as if
memories cannot also
kill you, as if being known
cannot, has not. another
train station. & besides,
who can say that david
did not tell his story,
tell it in full?

.

me. i say that. on that,

if nothing else, i will

stand firm. but i could be

the paleontologist who

placed the head on the wrong

end of the elasmosaurus,

made the neck the tail.

every detail i imbue with

meaning could be wrong.

a novelist at a murder scene

sounds like the setup

of a joke. the very impulse

to duck underneath the

yellow caution tape

& flip the notebook open

seems violently right &

violently wrong. perhaps

the particles must float in

solution, unreconciled,

suspended like judgment,

& my only job is to stare

at them the way i would the

tank of undulating jellyfish

at the aquarium, which

i also cannot understand,

but do not seek to.

this year i have been writing

con movies, the kind with a

final twist that makes you

think back & reconsider

every scene beforehand,

realize nothing was as

you'd believed. the mark

is always unsympathetic,

between the confidence

man's crosshairs because

he has no legal recourse, no

moral high ground upon

which to stand. he is

a cheater cheated, brought

low by his own duplicity,

his own bad faith.

there is no second act for

the mark. we never circle

back to see whether therapy

has helped him address

his nascent inability

to trust. the most we

grant him is a fleecing

so elegant that he never

realizes he's been had,

a brush-off that leaves

him thanking god he is

alive. it is intended

only as a precaution

against revenge, but

to live out your days

believing that misfortune

brought you low &

not deception, that

things might have

turned out far worse,

is no small grace,

makes me wish my

brother had contrived

to make us think he'd

drowned or been

hit by a bus & then

i am ashamed of

this thought, a plea for

erasure to multiply

itself.

.

we hardly speak of david
now. for years my mother
would erupt in tears if
anyone mentioned his
name, even her, so instead
he hovers in the periphery,
the space between words,
the rush to fill silences
however possible. when
we do talk about him it is
innocuous, incidental, my
dad recounting a museum
he took us to when we were
kids, never his death, never
the instructions he left us
about how to read his life.
for years i was my brother's
translator, the only one who
understood a word he said.

he threw tantrums because
he could not make clear what
he wanted, usually a spider-man
chewable vitamin. my parents
saw some vulnerability in him,
or else created it. he learned
to speak late & was not a
jailhouse lawyer when he did.
his intelligence clustered in
an unfamiliar quadrant,
was not fierce & literary
but curious, methodical, &
this was foreign, hard
to see at first. our schtick
was words, puns, opinions
legal & otherwise, we
did not suspend judgment
or embrace the scientific
method. we were generations

deep in trying to figure out

what to make of the strange

new freedom to do something

besides study the talmud all

fucking day but had not really

ventured very far afield.

by the time the realization

hit that david was maybe

the smartest of us all,

the odds had been set.

he had been handicapped.

i am not saying any

of this is a reason for

anything, just wondering

what it must have felt like.

they say that if somebody is

going to kill himself he'll

find a way. you can't stop it

by cutting off the means.

there is so much received

wisdom on this topic, so

many books that all say

the same thing, so many

vectors of exoneration.

but what if you had started

trying to stop him years

before, what then? surely

there is some juncture,

some inflection point at

which it is still possible,

despite what his note said.

& i am mortified to say that
only now does it occur to me
that david might have written
what he did to let his readers
off the hook, convince us
he never had a chance. that
both the notes he left behind
were about protecting
the living.

how early does the brain
subsume its fundamental
truths, begin to grow
around them like the knife
plunged into the heart
of a tree? what if he had
told someone besides his
wife? what if this person
had dragged him to a doctor

right away & what if

that doctor had made

david speak, confess

all, & then convinced

him that there was no

shame in it, made my

brother take pill after pill,

tweaking medicines &

dosages until the roiling

ocean of his brain chemistry

settled into steady three

foot swells or shimmering

placidity? what if this person

had been me?

the last time the world's

greatest drummer ever

drummed, i was there.

elvin ray jones had been in

hospital for six months,

his liver & kidneys shutting

down, avenging past

abuse, when keiko, his

wife & manager, my

former boss, called me.

she had pulled veen out,

against the doctor's orders,

& they were coming

to oakland to play yoshi's

& needed help. i'd left

new york a year before

& hadn't traveled with

them since, knew he'd

been sick but little more.

when i arrived i found veen

sitting alone in the dark

greenroom, forty pounds

lighter & already partway

somewhere else. he gave

me a papery hug & muttered

hard shit. dying, i think he

meant. the band was mostly

new cats, hastily assembled.

the only people who had

known him long were

delfeayo & me. elvin was

barely talking, but keiko

told me that in the hospital

he had spoken frequently

of john, whose name seldom

passed veen's lips in normal

times, the loss too raw despite

the years. when reporters

asked, veen fed them platitudes,

said john had been an angel

sent from heaven. i always

took this to mean that elvin

was the demon in their

partnership, elemental &

propulsive, the churning

ocean atop which coltrane

balanced as he searched

for god. there was an

oxygen tank now,

backstage at first & then,

as the week unfolded,

on it, tubes snaking from

behind the floor toms into

elvin's nostrils. the audience

did not know what to make

of what they saw. one night

the doctor who supplied

the tank got caught in traffic

& the tip of veen's right stick

came up half an inch short

of the golden ride cymbal

every time he tried to hit it.

every time. the fans were

in agony, doubled forward

in their chairs, willing the wood

to find the hammered metal.

i heard an old man say *let him*

go home & get some rest!

as if veen had been rousted

from the sickbed against his

will. but keiko knew exactly

what she was doing. elvin

had allowed her to see him,

in all his naked fullness,

& so when the time came

here he was, dying at home

on his drum stool. his purpose

had never been in doubt.

he was on the planet to

offer the gift of his music

to a world that needed

all the love & majesty those

songs contained. seldom

did a gig pass in all my years

sitting backstage with keiko

that she did not tell me

as much, restate this thesis,

eyes widening over her cup

of tea, bright painted lips

pursed as she nodded in

somber agreement with

herself. his job was to play

& hers was to make sure

that nothing stopped him,

to sweep away impediments

& master details, belay

danger no matter the source

or the toll it took. i saw her

throw musicians bodily

out of nightclubs when

they showed up on that

shit, because nobody high

was going to be alone

with keiko's husband ever

again. they were heroes to

each other, or perhaps figures

from one of the japanese

myths she turned into

songs for him to play:

the monk & his sworn

warrior protectress.

elvin's certitude sat at

the precise center of him,

radiating an electric peace

that, by the time it reached

his four extremities

& passed into the bass

& hi-hat, snare & toms

& crash & ride, became

a storm. the very last night,

keiko stood behind him

as he played the final

song of the first set,

arms wrapped around

his chest as if he were

her mask. the tune was

dear lord, one of john's.

when it was over, veen sat

motionless behind the trap

kit while we waited for

the room to clear. delfeayo

& i had to carry him

offstage, lift elvin beneath

the armpits & press our

hands against his back

as he labored to move

the same legs that had just

powered the pedals, his

smell still sharp & clean,

his forehead & medallion

glistening & the people

didn't need to see that.

but this time, as the house

lights rose, veen picked

his sticks up & began

to play. the crowd turned,

surged back inside, massed

before the stage. the sound

was thunderous, exalted,

the equal of any solo

i had ever heard him play,

& i had heard hundreds.

i wonder if it is possible that

what that solo was for elvin,

loosing those two gases &

allowing them to become

one & opening his lungs

was for my brother.

one day when he was

ninety-five, & eighteen

months into retirement,

my grandfather, being of

sound mind & body,

came to believe that he

would die tomorrow.

he told his home health

aide, whose name was

also david, that a statute

enshrined in massachusetts

state law mandated

the demise of any citizen

who reached an age

of ninety-five unless

he filed contravening

paperwork. ben had

neglected to do so, &

unless immediate action

was taken, he would not

survive the night. i arrived

to visit, & told him such

a thing could not be possible.

he explained that the statute

was unusual & began

describing it further,

employing the exquisite

phrasing for which his legal

writings were celebrated:

it was *intended to curtail*

the vitality of persons attaining

a certain advanced longevity.

i attempted to advance

some legalistic retorts

but knew i was outmatched even

before he waved me off,

a characteristic gesture,

said it was hard to explain

& i was not a lawyer,

a characteristic dismissal.

at this point an old colleague,

a fellow judge, chanced

to drop by, & he took up

the matter, tried to assuage

the old man's panic by

citing cruzan v. missouri,

the constitution itself,

issues of state & federal

jurisdiction, the quandary of

enforceability—opening

& abandoning fronts at

a fantastic rate but never

seeming to question

the precept that we had to

defeat this delusion on

legal grounds. my grandfather
acknowledged every point but
remained steadfast, terrified.
his inability to engender
belief seemed to puzzle
the old man, whose word
had always & often literally
been law. finally the other
judge rose, defeat hanging
from him like a scarf, &
took his leave. i reached
for ben's hand, told him
that i would fix this. my
throat tightened around
the words. in some strange
way, i believed my grandfather,
felt his life had become my
responsibility, welcomed it.
i left the room & returned

a few minutes later claiming

to have spoken to his lawyer

& been assured that all

the papers had been filed

with the court. ben narrowed

his eyes & my heart surged.

then he shook his head,

told me the lawyer was

mistaken. it was all i

could do not to scream

but these are your rules!

i withdrew to his study to

regroup. the air was heavy,

the clutter on the broad

mahogany desk that had

once been his father-in-law's

frozen in time. ben would

never pen another opinion

there, perhaps never so much

as set foot in this room again,

even if he lived another

decade. it was full of his

strength, his brilliance,

the strength & brilliance of

his generation. in this room,

he was already dead.

i sank into the low chair,

looked up at the leather

bound law books filling

the inlaid floor to ceiling

shelves. there had never

been a ladder, as if

all these volumes were

simply duplicate records

of the knowledge my

grandfather carried inside

him. the belief that i was

the man for this job had

vanished so thoroughly

it seemed remarkable i'd

ever held it. i had been

wrong to offer him false

hope, to try to help ben

litigate his way out when

the thing he was trying

to confront was that he

couldn't. i put the old man

to bed, told him i'd see him

in the morning, & went home.

i should have stayed. i should

have held his hand until

the statute took or spared

him. what might ben have

told me if i'd sat up with

him & waited, if both of us

had given up the fight,

accepted what was coming,

readied ourselves instead

of readying some feeble

defense? did i leave him

alone because i did not

believe i could be of any

solace, just as david

believed of us all, or

because i could not bear

his suffering, as david

could not bear his own &

could not bear to let us see?

it turned out to be

a urinary tract infection.

in the elderly, the bacteria

often beelines to the brain.

we got him on antibiotics

& by the next day

ben was immortal again.

he lived four more years

& never found a better

way to reckon with

the coming of the end.

when death arrived my

grandfather was no more

ready than he had been

that night, & the old man

did not go in peace. david

was ready, wholly &

horribly ready, but nor

did he. or did he? i cannot

know, & do not know

which one is worse.

they say the voice is

the first thing you forget,

but i can close my eyes

right now & hear david's

wobbly baritone on my

voicemail. *hey, it's your*

brother, or sometimes

hey champ, an inside

joke we'd borrowed

from our cousins without

ever bothering to understand.

i remember his weird outgoing

message, *you've reached*

david. how are you? he was

an awkward dude, not hard

to love but hard to feel

close to, hard to reach.

questions intended to elicit

feelings brought back

bloodless recitations of fact.

asperger's crossed my mind.

he adopted the traits &
eccentricities of relatives,
wove them jaggedly into
himself: my mother's exact
way of talking to dogs, my
taste in music, matthew's
taste in music, jeanette's
expressions, the angle
at which ben crossed
his legs. even the
appropriation of *hey*
champ was him, was
typical. he sometimes
seemed less a discrete
individual than a collage
of foibles, scotch-taped
together. the borrowed ones
were small. those unique
to david were outlandish,

out of proportion, shadow

puppets mimicking a

personality's volume & form.

in my fiction workshop they

would have been derided

as lazy, an end run around

character development: this

guy is the guy who wears

shorts even in a blizzard.

this guy is the guy who

insists he is a year older

than he is because his first

birthday was the day he

was born, & is not kidding,

& won't drop it. this guy

is either a brilliant &

twisted performance artist

deliberately boring you with

endless drivel about the settings

of his bread machine to
see how long you'll listen
or else he is not, & you can't
tell. all this is true & yet
unfair. my brother had
a core, & it was kindness,
learning for the sake of
learning, shoveling neighbors'
driveways, volunteering as a
hospital translator, mailing
care packages to the nuns
he'd befriended in nicaragua,
a gringo village saint. they
still write letters to my father.
i think we sent them all
his clothes. but in between
the bones & skin, the skeletal
system & the integumentary,
it sometimes seemed there lay

only a slurry of shredded masks,

a mulch of mirror shards, a tk

notation such as you might

find typed on the dedication

page of a bound manuscript

whose author cannot decide

who all this has been for.

vivien still does not know

how he died, this uncle she

cannot remember. when she

was five, i told her the story

of how he joined the polar

bear club one new year's day,

charged into the icy sea with

the rest of the crazy people,

the youngest of the bunch

by forty years. she listened

somberly, then asked if that

was why he died. i said no,

no, he was sick, & she has

not asked since. i take his

picture out, show her,

try to open the blinds,

let in some air, some light.

it should not be a mystery,

i cannot have this limning

the edges of her childhood,

curling them back like

burning newspaper.

i will have failed if his death

is the master key that

opens up her father when

at last i hand it over.

all she knows right now

is that she may not make

breezy jokes about killing

herself, as kids will do.

i have almost tipped

my hand, i think, jerking

the car onto the shoulder &

twisting backward in my seat

to forbid, forbade, my voice

more taut than i intend.

she can already lawyer
me to pieces, find the
loopholes in my language
& cannonball right through.
felicia would have adored
her. they cut with the same
blade & same panache,
rhythm to spare & puns to
order, orchestrators of activity,
collectors of people, players
of games of skill, lovers of
theater & theatrics. but what
came for david might very
well be hiding inside vivien.
an inheritance from ben.
from marion. from nights
of long knives & caves
of fire, simmering in the
deoxyribonucleic acid,

they say panic ruins

the meat, & her mother's

family is no better on this

score than mine. if this

thing is in my daughter,

if it passed clean through

me like a round shot from

a gun & found her, she

is going to need the words

my brother never had, the

words he could not even

leave behind. soon after

his death, my mother

tried to make me promise i

would never write about

david. i said nothing &

continued to say nothing

until now, & still do not

know if she asked because

it is nobody's business or

would be too painful to

see rendered on the page

or simply because when

my mother was a girl,

felicia promised never to

write about her & this,

she feels, is what a writer

owes his family. but i will

make a different plea to my

children. i will implore

them to write it, speak it

all. shed light & who knows

what else you might shed.

if i am lucky, the worst is

done. i did not realize

the good times were

the good times then

but i know eden now.

i have three beautiful
daughters like some
fucking farmer in a joke
& a partner i love &
goddamn it is all so
fragile. just outlive me,
all of you, that's all i
ask. let nature take
this round.

the things he gave me
are totemic & devoid
at once. a hand drum
from ahmedabad, a
costa rican hammock,
a cuban baseball jersey,
some low red candle
holders from the crate
& barrel outlet store,

a ginger grater he

swore by, a wooden

molinillo that was

a favor at his wedding,

a yerba maté gourd &

metal straw, a kurta pyjama.

on his birthday & the

anniversary of his death,

i gather a few into a pile

& think this, this is all i

have left or tell myself

i had a brother once.

on those days you cannot

wait for the levee to break,

you have to bash it yourself,

get it over with. there is no

hiding from dates. the body

recognizes the planet's

obliquity, the length of

the night, the sweetness

of the air, the pollen count.

i can feel april eighteen &

may twenty-eight coming

weeks away, my ribcage

swinging open like a fucking

advent calendar.

there was a time the mask

slipped, or rather a time i

tried to wrest it from my face.

it was two thousand

fourteen, during the brief

respite between mid april

& late may, & i was one of

five storytellers slated

to perform before a boston

theater packed full of public

radio enthusiasts. these stories,

i would come to realize,

followed an established arc.

the first few minutes were

fun & games, & then came

the turn: stories about marriage

became stories about cancer,

& then stories about how to

go on. stories about pregnancy

became stories about down

syndrome, & then stories

about how to go on. my piece

was the closer & nothing

about it matched. it was a

standup routine, essentially.

there was a turn, but it cued

laughter, not a gasp or hush.

the lesson learned was facile,

& even that served to set up

a punchline. we rehearsed

the night before & i heard

everybody else's. they were

all so brave, so honest, &

i walked back to my hotel room

feeling like a liar & a cheat.

my story was about the book,

a cavalcade of swift vignettes

describing sudden minor fame

& how being mistaken for

a parenting expert had

caused me to question my

own parenting, the grafted

on dilemma that resolved

at last into an opening scene:

adam co-hosts a fundraiser

with an actual sleep expert,

who badly misreads his

audience of rich donors

& presents a highly technical

slideshow that bores them

to distraction, while also &

perhaps inadvertently throwing

adam under the sleep training

bus. this cements adam's

feeling of fraudulence, but

then, the turn, he retires

to his suite & finds an email

from said expert, revealing

that, as he has just this moment

learned, his son is an old friend

of adam's from summer camp.

adam has only one memory of

the kid: that twenty-three years

earlier, the two of them were

arrested when adam ripped

the head off a lifesized

cardboard cutout of mc hammer

at the back bay tower records,

an act motivated not by theft,

though there was theft, but

a desire to defend the purity

of hip hop culture by decapitating

an intruder. the sleep expert

sprang adam & his son, guilty

only by association, & drove

adam home, & when present

day adam the fake parenting

expert puts this all together,

it becomes a balm for his

distress. perhaps, he muses,

the lesson, we are all

experts & we are all frauds,

since even the great &

powerful doctor made so

egregious an error in

judgment as allowing

his son to hang out

with me.

what was this claptrap? i

paced my hotel room unable

to fall asleep. it was

one thing to have worn

the mask in real time,

for the sake of my family

& future & in the name

of forging on, & quite

another to bound onstage

tomorrow & present this

bullshit version of

the recent past, erase

my brother as my brother

had erased himself, erase

my suffering as if my

brother had been right &

he had not destroyed us.
i knocked on the director's
door & told her i could not
do this, that i wanted to
rewrite my entire piece.
a narrative was buzzing
inside me: this was shaping
up to be a defining moment,
stirring as fuck, the scene
where the leading man stares
down at the speech he is
meant to deliver, crumples
it into a ball, speaks from
the heart instead & reclaims
his integrity, his soul. i would
stay up all night drafting, fingers
flying over keys, truth
splashing onto the page
until i was out from

beneath all this shit at last.

she told me it was out of

the question, that my job

tomorrow was to end

the show on a high note,

that they put these evenings

together very carefully.

i nodded, left, took a long

cold walk through a city

i no longer knew. part of me

felt thwarted & another

was relieved. i told the story

& it killed, then told it

in another dozen cities.

i wrote three comedy books,

five middle-grade novels,

two supernatural thrillers, a

screenplay that became a movie,

three or four more that did not,

three tv pilots. i never broke
a sweat. i talked about writing
something serious, another
novel, the way a man who
isn't leaving his wife talks
about leaving his wife. i said
i knew i had to write about my
brother somehow, & daniel
& begley & kev listened
patiently, year after year.
david's widow met someone,
had a daughter. my parents
started laughing again, though
they still refuse to celebrate
birthdays, as if to do so
would constitute betrayal.
there is a gravestone for
david now, though his body
does not lie beneath it, on

martha's vineyard next to
felicia & ben, about whom
the running joke is that now
they can lie there not speaking
to each other forever. the mc
hammer story had been on
the radio by the time i
told it onstage at a private
club in san francisco the
night i met jamie. we went
out for drinks a week later,
putting an end to a run of
not dating jews that began
the year i should have been
bar mitzvahed. i told her
about david within half an
hour, before we even made
the commitment to move
from the bar to the table,

& it felt simple, clean,

nothing more or less

than the act of a person

wanting to be known.

this is beginning to

feel like an epilogue,

white titles flashing

on a black screen,

loose ends weaving

themselves into bows,

the score cresting in a

reprise of the theme as

coats are gathered &

phones thumbed back on.

that's not what i intend,

& who knows if writing

this will help or hurt, or

help as much as it hurts,

whether this is ritual

enough or ritual at all.

i have a weakness for

stories that end with

stories being written,

characters revealed as

authors, taking control

of their own narratives,

but that should not be this.

david took control, it could

be argued, & i can find

no peace in that, cannot

agree inside any more

than i can argue outwardly

when my mother, perhaps

seeking to wall off other

kinds of conversations, or

wring what comfort she can

from the desert of her grief,

says he must have been in

so much pain, as if this is

the final word, & why not,

she is right, it is true even

if we can only guess at

the shape & weight of

that pain, can never know

what it was like for him,

as him, & something

must be the final word,

why not say the kaddish.

holy shit—we did that.

i had totally forgotten.

the first year after david

died we gathered all the

california people, some

of whom had slipped through

the phone chain & still did not

know, just as i had feared.

they came to the house &

the oldest jew i could find

recited the prayer of mourning

& i don't know if it ripped me

open or soldered me shut. but

you were mourned for, david,

you were loved, you are loved

& mourned for still, you

cannot leave entirely,

i will not let you go.

acknowledgments

Kevin Coval. Daniel Alarcón.
Sarah Suzuki. Josh Begley.
Idris Goodwin. W. Kamau Bell.
Adam Lazarus. Mitch Zuckoff.
Kathryn Borel. Sheila Heti.
Kristin Campbell. Joan Morgan.
Elizabeth Méndez Berry. DJ Frane.
Chris Jackson. Andre C. Willis.
Richard Abate. Johnny Temple.
Ricardo Cortés. Oliver Wang.
Eli Epstein. Jeff Chang.
Torrance Rogers. Bryant Terry.
Weyland Southon. Davey D.
Sy Kaufman. Neil Drumming.
Eugene Cho. Theo Gangi.
Andrew Bujalski. Dave Cohen.
Jean Grae. Danny Hoch.
Chinaka Hodge. Mark Johnson.
Douglas Mcgowan. Josh Lenn.

Thomas Fraser. Dug Infinite.
Mark Pellington. Blake Lethem.
Sophia Chang. Emery Petchauer.
Nate Marshall. Angel Nafis.
Courtney Morris. Martín Perna.
Vinnie Wilhelm. Zoe Wilhelm.
J.Period. Lauren A. Whitehead.
Josh Healey. Jason Santiago.
Joe Schloss. Rachael Knight.
Marc Bamuthi Joseph. Dave Barry.
Kamy Wicoff. Matthew Kaplan.
Alan Zweibel. Matthew Zapruder.
Charlie Mansbach. Nancy Mansbach.
Vivien Mansbach. Zanthe Mansbach.
Asa Mansbach. Jamie Greenwood,
most of all.

These people helped me write this book. Some got me
through the earliest days of grief & shock, or the later
ones. Others read parts of this manuscript & offered
insight & support, or talked through with me, over the
course of years, how I might write this, or inspired me
to try at all. I am grateful, deeply grateful, to them all.

about the author

ADAM MANSBACH is a novelist, screen-writer, cultural critic, and humorist. He is the author of the #1 *New York Times* bestsellers *Go the Fuck to Sleep,* which has been translated into forty languages and has sold more than three million copies worldwide, and the 2014 sequel, *You Have to Fucking Eat.* His novels include *Rage Is Back, Angry Black White Boy,* and *The End of the Jews,* winner of the California Book Award.

adammansbach.com
Facebook.com/adam.mansbach
Twitter: @adammansbach
Instagram: @adammansbach